FACING IMMIGRATION PROBLEMS?

Helpful Answers To Common Immigration Issues

By Paris Lee, Esq.

ISBN: 978-1-941645-09-3

Design and Published by:

Speakeasy Marketing, Inc.
73-03 Bell Blvd #10
Oakland Gardens, NY 11364

www.SpeakeasyMarketingInc.com
(888) 225-8594

DISCLAIMER

This publication is intended to be informational only. No legal advice is being given, and no attorney-client relationship is intended to be created by reading this material. If you are facing legal issues, please seek professional legal counsel to get your questions answered.

LEE & GARASIA, LLC.

190 State Route 27
Edison, NJ 08820
(732) 516-1717
(888) 404-5876

www.njimmigrationattorney.com

Client Testimonials

"Lee and Garasia are excellent lawyers, punctual and professional. They are dedicated to going above and beyond the usual level of service to meet your client's needs. Their staff is very knowledgeable, friendly and polite. I would highly recommend this firm to anyone." **-Madie B.**

……………………………………………………………...

"My wife and I had complicated case for US Citizen application. We could not do it without Mr. Lee and Ms. Garasia's professional help. Mr. Lee gave us straight answers and honest advice. We could not be happier that we had Ms. Garasia accompany us for interview. She is the best. She knows exactly what to do and say at the right time to keep interview smoothly and protect our rights at the same time. I recommend this firm to all my relatives and friends who will need legal help in immigration in the future." **- Robert C.**

……………………………………………………………...

I can't thank you enough for all the hard work, effort and dedication you put into my case. I wouldn't be where I am today without your help. You have changed my life! Thank you VERY much! **-Shereen A.**

……………………………………………………………...

Thank you for making my case go smooth, easy and quick. I appreciate your assistance. It was appreciated more than you know..... **-Mr. & Mrs. Brown**

TABLE OF CONTENTS

ATTORNEY INTRODUCTION

Paris Lee is Founding Partner of Lee and Garasia, LLC, one of New Jersey's most prominent immigration law firms. Mr. Lee has over 17 years legal experience and is admitted to practice law in New Jersey and Washington, D.C. He is an alumnus of The Lawrenceville School as well as a graduate of Yale University and Rutgers School of Law (Newark).

Prior to starting Lee and Garasia, LLC, Mr. Lee clerked for the Monmouth County Prosecutor's Office in Freehold, New Jersey, prosecuting municipal appeals and preparing briefs on a wide array of criminal issues involving search and seizure as well as the constitutionality of the death penalty. After his stint there, Mr. Lee practiced criminal defense in addition to and alongside immigration, handling cases on both the New Jersey Municipal and Superior Court levels. He has appeared in nearly every county of New Jersey representing clients charged with traffic and quasi-criminal offenses from speeding to shoplifting to assault.

As an immigration law attorney, Mr. Lee chairs the litigation department. Besides managing and directing the adjustment of status and consular visa sections of the practice, he represents clients in Immigration Court and is responsible for preparing Waivers, Appeals, Motions to Reopen, and Deferred Action Requests.

Mr. Lee is a member of AILA (The American Immigration Lawyers Association), the New Jersey State Bar Association (Chair-Elect, Immigration and Naturalization Section), Middlesex County Bar Association (Co-Chair, Immigration Law and Practice Committee), Federal Bar Association, and the Association of Criminal Defense Lawyers-NJ.

He is also nationally recognized for his expertise in immigration law and was featured in Newsweek's 2013 Nationwide Top Attorneys Showcase and TIME Magazine as a Leader in Immigration Law.

He is a Black Belt in Brazilian Jiu-Jitsu under Renzo and Rolles Gracie.

A Broad Client Base

Interviewer: What kinds of people come to you? Is it just your typical foreign national that's visiting here, or is it an undocumented person staying here illegally with other family members?

Paris Lee: Our client base is very broad. We basically serve three discrete groups of people. The first category is comprised of people who are already lawful permanent residents (or "green card" holders) who want to become citizens. We help them navigate the process of naturalization: from determining eligibility to filling out the necessary forms to appearing at the interview.

The second group are people who are already US citizens who want to file for their foreign born spouses or family members. These relatives may already be present within the United States or living abroad. Depending on where they are, that will determine which process we file under. In some cases, we will help them to file for adjustment of status, and in other cases, initiate a consular processing case. The last group are people who have problems with their status. Some may have entered the country illegally, some may have overstayed, some may already be in Immigration Court. In any case, these people are collectively considered "undocumented" or "illegal." Our job, of course, is to properly advise them and help them, if possible, fix their status.

And there's actually another group: our "crimmigration" clients. These are people who are not US Citizens who get involved with the criminal justice system somehow, whether it's a misdemeanor or a felony charge. We often have to assess what the immigration consequences are if they have to plead guilty to something.

Interviewer: In general, what are the largest ethnic groups that you tend to work with?

Paris Lee: I have a pretty broad range of ethnicities. Perhaps because of where we are located, we tend to serve a large Indian clientele, but we help people from many different cultures and backgrounds.

Interviewer: In your practice, what languages do you speak besides English, if any? Do you have any associates that speak other languages?

Paris Lee: My partner is originally from India so she speaks a dialect called Gujarati. In our office, I have staff that are multilingual, so we are also able to accommodate people who speak Spanish, Hindi, and even Turkish.

Provisional Unlawful Presence Waiver Program

Interviewer: We'll start with people that are either already citizens or are already here legally. They want to bring over a family member – brother or sister or something like that. A couple of things I've seen is one must go about a provisional unlawful presence waiver. What is that and what does it tell our people to do?

Paris Lee: This is something that's a relatively new program that USCIS implemented last year. It came out in March of 2013. While not exactly amnesty, it is perhaps one of the best things we currently have in the way of progressive immigration reform. Basically, the program is aimed at helping people who cannot adjust their status here leave and come back with their immigrant visas. It is only available at this time to Immediate Relatives of United States citizens who can prove extreme hardship to a US Citizen spouse or parent.

Interviewer: Well, what's a waiver and how does it work?

Paris Lee: Let's say, for example, that somebody came in through the border without inspection. He/she sneaks in but later on gets married to a US citizen. Under most circumstances—under the law as it is right now—these types of people would not be able to file for their green cards within the United States. They're ineligible to do so.

A person in this type of situation would actually have to leave the country and apply for an immigrant visa at the US consulate in his/her native country to reenter the United States. However, the problem is that once he/she departs from the United States, a 3 or 10-year unlawful presence bar is potentially triggered. So, in practical terms, if the person leaves, he is she is stuck outside for possibly 10 years. The only way to get around the bar is to file for a waiver. You are essentially asking immigration to forgive you and cancel the 10-year bar so that you may re-enter the United States. For the traditional unlawful presence waiver, you have to demonstrate extreme hardship to a US citizen or lawful permanent resident spouse or parent. If the waiver is approved, the person will be allowed to reenter. However, if the waiver is denied, that person is out of luck: he or she will be stranded outside until the bar no longer applies.

The Provisional Waiver Program Allows Ineligible People to File for a Waiver Within The United States

What the provisional waiver program does is basically allow people ineligible to file for adjustment of status--but subject to the bar--to file for the waiver within the United States, as opposed to filing the waiver outside the United States. This can mean a world of a difference to families facing separaton because it eliminates some of the uncertainty and anxiety involved with leaving the country not knowing what will happen. Of course, if the waiver is approved, the intending immigrant still has to go outside the country for an interview at the US consulate, but the point is that if the person goes under these circumstances, he or she can reasonably feel confident in being able to return to the US because the problem has already been addressed and resolved with US Citizenship and Immigration Services (USCIS). Conversely, if the waiver is not granted, the person would not even be leaving because there would obviously be no point to doing so.

Interviewer: What will happen if it's not granted? Will the government go after the person?

Paris Lee: Under most circumstances, no. What people need to understand is that there is USCIS, which is in charge of benefits, and there is ICE – Immigration and

Customs Enforcement – which is in charge of enforcement. When you apply for a provisional waiver, you are applying for the waiver through USCIS. If USCIS denies the waiver, it is not going to refer the case or inform ICE unless you meet the criteria for referral—which in most cases, means that you have a criminal record, committed some sort of fraud, or are seen as a threat to national security.

If you were to fall into those three types of categories, then, yes, there is a risk that you might be exposed because USCIS would refer the case to ICE. On the other hand, if you *did* fall into those types of categories, I don't think any ethical attorney who knows the ins and outs of immigration law would be recommending the provisional waiver in the first place.

Interviewer: It sounds like out of the three classifications, the fraud ones would be the easiest for people to do.

Paris Lee: Unfortunately, yes. If somebody has submitted false information or made any misrepresentation in connection with an immigration application, he or she is at risk of not only being denied but referred for removal proceedings. The provisional waiver program is strictly for people whose only problem is that they are in the United States illegally and would be subject to the unlawful presence bar if they left. If they have committed any fraud or misrepresentation in connection with an immigration application, they would likely be ineligible for the provisional waiver program. They would unfortunately have to leave the United States and file for whatever waivers are necessary (such as the unlawful presence *and* fraud waivers) from outside.

Interviewer: It seems like a very high stakes, nerve-wracking type of thing to do, even though the rules have changed for some lucky people. How do you get people to do this?

Paris Lee: Well, it is not something to be taken lightly. The decision to do a waiver requires some foresight, planning, and a bit of optimism. A waiver also requires a considerable investment of time and money, with no guarantee that it will be granted.

But on the other hand, with the way things are going, immigration reform may or may not materialize. A lot of people are making the choice to apply because they are not hopeful that something will pass and this is the most realistic option to fix their status. Unless they fall into a category of people that might be exposed to removal proceedings if the waiver were to be denied, it is worth taking the chance because an approval can change their life dramatically.

Common Mistakes in Applying for the Provisional Waiver Program

Interviewer: In this scenario, what are the top mistakes people make unintentionally that hurt their ability to apply for a waiver?

Paris Lee: The most common mistake is not understanding the eligibility requirements. Not everyone can apply for this type of waiver. If you want to file for the waiver, you have to be an immediate relative. What that means is that you have to be the spouse, child, or parent of a US citizen. You must also demonstrate extreme hardship, but you can only demonstrate extreme hardship to a US citizen spouse or parent.

Lawful permanent resident spouse or parents, or even US citizen children are not qualifying relatives. You can only show hardship to a US citizen spouse or parent for purposes of the provisional waiver program. If you're filing under the regular waiver program, then the categories of qualifying relatives are a little bit broader but for the *provisional* waiver program, it's limited to US citizens spouses or parents.

Also, another thing that has to be recognized is that it still involves the individual having to leave the United States. Some people are under the impression that the waiver allows to them to just fix their status from within United States. It doesn't do that. The person still has to leave the United States and go to the US consulate in their native country to apply for a visa to come back. The waiver only eliminates the unlawful presence bar, but the person is not going to be allowed to just stay in the United States and take care of everything here without having to leave. It is "provisional" because you are getting an answer to your application here in the US before an interview abroad is even scheduled.

Interviewer: But legally, if it's approved, it's okay and there's probably a high likelihood of coming back.

Paris Lee: Yes, if the waiver has been approved because the issue of unlawful presence and its consequences has already been addressed and resolved by USCIS.

Interviewer: Right, because otherwise it's like a nasty trick.

Paris Lee: Yes, exactly. It would be a particularly cruel ruse to get the person to leave and then tell him/her that he or she is barred for 10 years. No, it's not supposed to work like that.

If the waiver gets approved, you're going to be able to go and come right back. (But again, this is provided that unlawful presence is the only issue.)

Timeframe of Provisional Waiver Applications

Interviewer: Can you give any ballpark figure as to how long the process takes?

Paris Lee: Understand that we are only estimating, and that every case is different, but a case that involves the filing of a provisional waiver can take approximately a year and a half. (A regular consular process by itself, without a waiver, takes approximately one year if the Beneficiary is an immediate relative.)

Extreme Hardship

Interviewer: What is an example of extreme hardship?

Paris Lee: There is no concrete definition. The whole process can be quite subjective. Basically what you have to demonstrate is that whoever the qualifying relative is going to be – whether it's a US citizen spouse or a US citizen parent – you have to show how they're going to suffer without the presence of the foreign national here.

For example, if the foreign national is the sole means of financial support to the US relative, what would happen if he or she were not allowed to come back for ten years? How would the US Citizen support him or herself if he or she is disabled or been out of the workforce? Or maybe there is a medical issue. If the US Citizen has some sort of illness and is receiving treatment here in the US, would he or she receive comparable treatment in the foreign natonal's country?

You have to show how the qualifying relative is going to suffer without the foreign national here in the US *and* how that person is going to suffer if he/she were to travel abroad with the foreign national. You have to address both points.

Political Instability

Interviewer: What if the person was from a politically unstable country?

Paris Lee: That's also another consideration. If the intending immigrant's native country is a dangerous place to live, it might constitute extreme hardship for the qualifying relative to go live there and risk his/her safety.

FRAUD OR CRIMINAL RECORD

Interviewer: What are some of the reasons that someone would have a fraud or criminal issue that would block him or her from getting this waiver ?

Paris Lee: When we are discussing whether someone is eligible for permanent residence, we must always consider issues of admissibility. If you have a criminal conviction, especially for a crime that is classified as one involving moral turptitude, you would not only be ineligible for the provisional waiver, but you may be ineligible to even apply for a green card.

What is a crime involving moral turpitude? That's avery nebulous term. There is no strict definition but basically it's a crime that somebody commits knowingly and generally one that is against the common morality and norms of society. Generally speaking, crimes such as shoplifting, aggravated assault or theft by deception are ones that are considered to involve moral turpitude. If someone has a crime involving moral turpitude in his/her history, he or she not only needs to worry about the consequences of unlawful presence but also the ramifications of the conviction.

Interviewer: Shoplifting and aggravated assault are pretty different offenses.

Paris Lee: Yes, but that gives you an idea of how broad the range of offenses can be that might jeopardize an application for permanent residence. Everything is very case and statute sensitive. That's why we have cases where we have to help advise foreign-born criminal defendants of the potential impact of a criminal charge or convicton. A lot of people, unfortunately, plead guilty not knowing that by pleading guilty, they are actually ruining their chances of one day qualifying for permanent residence, especially if a waiver is not applicable.

Interviewer: What about fraud and criminal waivers? How does that play into it?

Paris Lee: If you've committed any type of fraud or any type of misrepresentation in applying for an immigration benefit, or if you have a criminal conviction that renders you inadmissible to the United States, you may need to explore whether you can file for a waiver of those grounds.

There are two different waivers.

There is the 212i waiver that may be available to waive fraud and misrepresentation. There is also the 212h waiver to waive certain criminal convictions. They each respectively have their own requirements, but generally speaking, the principle is the same. You're going to have to demonstrate extreme hardship to a qualifying relative. In some cases it's going to be a US citizen or a permanent resident, spouse or parent. In other cases, it could potentially be a US citizen or permanent resident spouse, parent or child.

Interviewer: How easy is it to get this waiver and how tough is it to get if you've already pled guilty to a crime and been convicted of one?

Paris Lee: Waivers are difficult, but not impossible, to get approved. They require a lot of time and extensive documentation. Depending on what your factor is going to be, whether it's a medical issue or financial circumstances, or a combination of those things, you have to assemble documentation to back your theory. For example, if the US citizen spouse has a medical problem – let's say hypothetically, he/she is suffering from cancer – you have to prove that. You have to get medical records to corroborate what the person is suffering from. You also might have to demonstrate how that type of treatment is not available in the foreign national's country.

If you're talking about financial issues, if the foreign national is the one who is making most of the money and supporting the qualifying relative, then you have to substantiate that. You're going to have to show what the monthly budget of the family is and how much the foreign national makes and what would happen if that foreign national's income was no longer included in the picture.

Interviewer: For a fraud or crime waiver, what kind of people do you see that have to apply for these cases? What are their reasons?

Paris Lee: Let's pretend that an individual came here on a visitor's visa and overstayed but subsequently married a US citizen. Let's also assume that he has a bona fide, true relationship with his wife, and that the wife files for his green card. If that person has ever been convicted of a serious crime involving moral turpitude, even if it happened decades ago, he may be deemed inadmissible. In this type of scenario, he is going to have to file for a waiver so that immigration may forgive or overlook the conviction.

But to answer your question: the people who normally have to file criminal waivers—at least the ones that I run into—are ordinary people like you or me who have made mistakes in the past but are now much different people.

They are married, have been for years, and may have families.

Interviewer: What about fraud waivers? Do they go through USCIS or ICE?

Paris Lee: They go through USCIS.

Interviewer: But are they more likely to be reported to ICE?

Paris Lee: Depends. It depends on how serious and material the fraud is, and whether USCIS feels that a referral is appropriate under the circumstanes.

Interviewer: So would you say that a fraud or criminal waiver is actually more dangerous to apply for than an unlawful presence waiver?

Paris Lee: Possibly. Of course, it depends on the case. You have to be very careful before you consider applying to immigration for anything because when you apply, you are, in a sense, exposing yourself. It could certainly backfire and if it backfires, you might find yourself in removal proceedings.

Removal Proceedings (Deportation)

Interviewer: Would you be able to help people who end up in removal proceedings? Or does that mean it's pretty much over for them?

Paris Lee: Yes, we represent people in removal proceedings before the Immigration Court. Of course, it's a totally different venue with different rules, but just because you are in removal proceedings does not mean that you will be deported. Removal proceedings are court proceedings. You do have certain rights. The government is going to have to prove that you are deportable. There may be certain forms of relief that you qualify for. For example, if the government is alleging that you are deportable because you've been convicted of a crime involving moral turpitude, we might be able to argue in court that that particular conviction is not a crime of moral turpitude.

Even if an individual is deportable, he/she still might qualify for certain forms of relief. For example, there is something called cancellation of removal. There's actually two types of cancellation: one for lawful permanent residents and one for nonpermanent residents.

The point is that even though you may be in Immigration Court, it doesn't mean that that's the end of the road; obviously you are in jeopardy, but there might be some things that you could apply for to still possibly stay here.

CRIME & IMMIGRATION

Interviewer: When people are charged with crimes, is it better if they go for an immigration attorney to represent them or do they need two attorneys –a criminal one and an immigration one as a specialist?

Paris Lee: Ideally, unless the immigration attorney also has experience in criminal law (which I do), you're going to need two attorneys. You're going to need a very skilled criminal defense attorney

but if you're not a US citizen, you will also need to have an immigration attorney involved as well. This is so that the immigration attorney can assess whether the criminal defense lawyer's strategy is consistent with the client's immigration goals.

Interviewer: Do you consult with criminal attorneys to handle immigration consequences on a regular basis?

Paris Lee: I do, yes, even more so now because of a Supreme Court case called *Padilla v. Kentucky* which mandates foreign national criminal defendants need to be advised of the immigration conseqeunces of their pleas. If the criminal defense attorney is not aware of or unsure of the consequences, then he/she has to at the very least, advise the client to consult with an immigration attorney.

I have a lot of cases where I work with criminal defense attorneys to assess the immigration conseqences. Often times, a proposed plea will have an immigration impact, so what we try to do, in conjunction with the defense attorney, is to work out an alternative plea that doesn't.

Common Criminal Offenses With Immigration Consequences

Interviewer: What are the most common crimes where you're called in to help evaluate the immigration consequences?

Paris Lee: In New Jersey, in my practice, the most common type of crimes where I am asked to render an opinion are shoplifting, theft, theft by deception, assault, aggravated assault, terroristic threats, and criminal mischief. It runs the whole gamut really.

Interviewer: What about drugs?

Paris Lee: Drug crimes as well, yes. Possession of marijuana, distribution of marijuana, possession of paraphernalia – those are very common offenses as well.

Disclosure of Consequences

Interviewer: At what point will someone realize they have a problem if they are in court for a crime? When will the immigration issues surface – when it's done, or in the beginning?

Paris Lee: These days, especially in New Jersey, when you've been charged with a crime and you have to appear in court, the judge will advise you that if you are not a US citizen, you may need to consult with an immigration attorney. That's when a defendant normally first becomes aware. If not at that juncture, then hopefully the defense attorney will raise the issue of citizenship with the client.

Interviewer: Do you have people that get through the whole criminal process – they will be convicted and they think they're okay– but then all of a sudden ICE picks them up?

Paris Lee: Yes, absolutely. We have cases like that as well. There are plenty of people who, for whatever reason – maybe their defense attorneys never asked them whether they were US citizens or never discussed the immigration consequences – have gone ahead and pled guilty to crimes that render them deportable. The problem may not have been apparent at that time. It might come up years later when the person applies to renew the green card or apply for naturalization. Then it becomes a big problem.

Another context in which we see these ticking time bombs is when the people who have pled guilty decide to travel outside the US. They may be deemed inadmissible upon their return.

In cases like these, we sometimes have to try to reopen the original criminal case to vacate the conviction because the client was not properly advised of the immigration consequences of pleading guilty. If the client had known what pleading guilty really meant—he/she would become deportable or lose permanent residence—he/she would have rejected the plea agreement.

ICE & IMMIGRATION COURT

Interviewer: By going into the criminal process, is ICE automatically alerted?

Paris Lee: Under certain circumstances, ICE is alerted, especially if the person is incarcerated or charged with a serious indicatable offense; What ICE will normally do is place a detainer on the alien so that custody may be transferred to the Department of Homeland Security once the alien finishes the criminal sentence.

Interviewer: Are there special immigration jails?

Paris Lee: There are in New Jersey. Yes, there is an immigration facility that holds inmates for immigration court. Some people are also held in county jails or state prisons.

Interviewer: Can you work with someone at any stage of a removal hearing? Is there a point when it's too late?

Paris Lee: If somebody is in jeopardy of being deported from the country, we ideally want to be involved from the very beginning. If they lose their immigration court case, we can possibly appeal the case to the Board of Immigration Appeals.

DREAM Act/Deferred Action for Childhood Arrivals

Interviewer: What is DREAM/deferred action?

Paris Lee: DREAM/deferred action is something that protects young people who came into the country before the age of 16 and who meet certain requirements, (ie., possess a high school degree, have been continuously present since 2007, no criminal record, etc.) . A grant of deferred action under this program provides a two-year window of protection from removal proceedings as well as two years of work authorization.

This is of enormous utility to people who, through no fault of their own, came here as minors. These types of individuals practically grow up here, go through the high school system and graduate-- but then find that they really can't do much here because they're out of status. This program allows them to at least live their lives without fear of deportation and make some headway towards their future. It allows them to work in the United

States with authorization, as opposed to working illegally.

Interviewer: Could deferred status serve as a stepping stone to a green card?

Paris Lee: Possibly, yes. Congress has yet to pass any sweeping comprehensive immigration reform, but I suspect, or at least hope, that if something does pass one day, there will be some favorable provisions for "dreamers." There was talk of an accelerated path to permanent residence and ultimately, citizenship, but thus far, nothing has materialized.

Interviewer: Who tends to approach you for the deferred action program – the parents or the young adults themselves?

Paris Lee: Both. Some young adults approach me by themselves on their own initiative. In other cases, I am contacted by the parents who are aware of "DACA" (Deferred Action for Childhood Arrival) and obviously want what's best for their kids.

Interviewer: How long as Deferred Action for Childhood Arrivals been out? Is it too late to apply?

Paris Lee: This program came out in 2012, so it's been around. We're getting close to two years now and in fact, for many people, it will be time to renew. It's not too late to apply. As long as you meet the requirements, you can apply for an initial grant. If you already have it, and there are no material circumstances that would affect or change your eligibility, you would be able to renew it.

Interviewer: Can things go wrong?

Paris Lee: Yes, things can go wrong. If the individual has a serious criminal record and applies, it could backfire. Not only can the case be denied but the person might be referred for immigration proceedings. Of course, every situation is case sensitive, but the point is, any individual with special circumstances (such as a criminal record, false claim of citizenship, etc.) owes it to him/herself to get an evaluation done before submitting a DACA application. You certainly don't want to find out after you've applied and been denied that your case has been referred to Immigration and Customs Enforcement for further action.

Interviewer: That would be terrible.

Paris Lee: Yes, but that's the thing: sometimes individuals may not be aware that it's actually more complicated than it appears. For example, if they've been here for a while, they might have procured a social security number, but if they obtained the number through fraud, there might be an issue there. Similarly, if he or she has ever pretended or claimed to be a US Citizen, that could impact the application.

The Process of Naturalization

Interviewer: What is the naturalization process, and what does that mean?

Paris Lee: Well, first off, people need to understand that there is a difference between filing for permanent residence and filing for citizenship--they're not the same thing. Permanent residence basically allows the person to stay here indefinitely, as opposed to somebody who comes here on a visitor's visa, who would only be allowed to stay here for a limited period of time.

A naturalized U.S. Citizen, on the other hand, enjoys certain rights and privileges beyond the ability to stay in the US as long as he/she wants. With a US citizenship, you're allowed to vote. You can never be deported. You can travel outside for as long you want. There are numerous benefits to becoming a citizen, but of course, you generally need to be a permanent resident first before you can apply for naturalization.

Interviewer: Naturalization is the process by which you apply to become a US citizen.

Paris Lee: Correct. Exactly. Naturalization is for somebody who is already a permanent resident who now wishes to become a US citizen. The process involves filing the N-400 and meeting certain requirements of course, such as continuous presence, physical presence, good moral character, ability to speak and understand English, and knowledge of American history. This is all demonstrated at the citizenship interview.

Timeframe of Naturalization

Interviewer: How long is the naturalization process and what's involved?

Paris Lee: The naturalization process these days (as of June 2014) is taking approximately three to five months. After filing the application, the applicant will be ordinarily be scheduled for fingerprints and eventually called in for an interview where an immigration officer will review the application and administer the history test.

ELIGIBILITY FOR NATURALIZATION

Interviewer: What are some requirements that people may not know about?

Paris Lee: In most cases, you have to be a permanent resident for five years. There are certain circumstances where you can apply for naturalization after three years– that is, if you have been married and living in marital union with a U.S. Citizen spouse for three years (and the U.S. Citizen spouse has been a citizen for those three years).

A separate requirement is that you have to be physically present in the United States. So, someone who has traveled extensively outside the US, especially on trips that are six months or more, may have issues.

And of course, if you've ever been arrested or convicted of a crime, that also might disqualify you from naturalization because it potentially impacts your ability to demonstrate good moral character.

Interviewer: What if you have filed for bankruptcy or been involved in a lawsuit or had other financial troubles--would that disqualify you?

Paris Lee: Financial trouble, in and of itself, probably won't disqualify you, but at the same time, anything that reflects on your character could have an impact. There are situations, for example, where somebody is behind on taxes or just hasn't filed taxes (when they should have been filed). If you haven't filed your taxes when you were legally obligated to, that could lead to a finding that you don't have good moral character. This particular topic involves a lot of discretion on the officer's part. If you can demonstrate or prove that you on a payment plan with the IRS and you're making efforts to pay that balance, the officer might take that into consideration and still possibly approve your case.

Interviewer: Those are some unexpected things that people might not have already taken care of when they want to apply.

Paris Lee: Another area that men, in particular, neglect to look into before applying is whether they registered for the selective service. Believe it or not, there are many men out there who, for whatever reason – maybe they weren't aware of their obligation or maybe nobody told them – did not register with the selective service when they were supposed to, which is the law. If you don't register with the selective service, that could be a negative factor upon which a denial could be based.

Interviewer: What happens if you register to vote?

Paris Lee: If you register to vote and you are not a US citizen, you may have just rendered yourself deportable. This is a very sensitive topic, but in this type of scenario, your naturalization application may not only be denied but you may also be referred for removal proceedings unless you can demonstrate that you fall under the exception.

The same thing is true if you have ever claimed to be a United States citizen when you were not –such a finding or determination by an immigration officer could be disastrous and severely impact not only a citizenship application but more imporatantly, the person's ability to stay here.

Other Family Immigration Concerns

Interviewer: What other type of family immigration issues do you deal with very commonly?

Paris Lee: Besides, of course, being able to file for your spouse, a lot of family members want to file for their children. If you are a US citizen, you can file for your children who are over 21. If they're married, they're going to fall into under a certain category. If they're unmarried, they're going to fall into under a different category.

As a US citizen, you may also file for your siblings. The sibling category is the fourth preference category, which unfortuanately, seems to be taking the longest. Currently, it takes more than 10 years for a brother or sister of a US citizen to immigrate here.

If you are a lawful permanent resident, you can file for children under, as well as over, the age of 21, provided they remain single. There is no category for married children of lawful permanent residents. It is not uncommon for me to have to break the bad news to somebody that his/her adult son will not be able to immigrate through the parent petition because the marriage effectively cancelled the case.

Interviewer: I didn't realize that.

Paris Lee: Yes, a lot of unsuspecting folks don't find out until later. As the day gets closer, they're thinking, "Oh, my son is going to be able to come very soon." They tell me, "I want my son to come here. This is the date that we filed. It looks like the date is coming up. What else do we have to do?" Then when I discover that that son is married and the marriage took place while they were still permanent residents, not US citizens.

TYPES OF CITIZENSHIP

Interviewer: What about naturalized citizens versus people that are born here?

Paris Lee: Naturalized citizens, for the most part, have the same rights and privileges as people who are born here.

Interviewer: Are there any differences?

Paris Lee: There might be. I believe that you won't be able to run for President if you're a naturalized citizen.

Other than that, you virtually have the same rights and privileges, as well as responsibilities, that ordinary citizens have.

Incidentally, a lot of people who are already citizens by operation of law may not even be aware of it. These types of people would or should not be filing for naturalization *because they are already citizens*. Instead, they should be filing for a Certificate of Citizenship on Form N-600.

Did you know that there are also ways to derive your U.S. Citizenship? For example, if you are a child under the age of 18, you have your permanent residence already, and your parent naturalizes before you turn 18, you may have already become a United States citizen the same time your parent did, by operation of law.

Interviewer: What if you're born here to foreign nationals that aren't permanent residents? What does that make you?

Paris Lee: If you're born here, then you are automatically a U.S. citizen. If you're born abroad to a U.S. citizen, then under certain conditions, you may also already be a citizen. There are very specific rules that apply to different time periods. If you were born abroad to a U.S. citizen, you have to look at when you were born and what rules apply for that time period. If you are lucky enough, you may have become a U.S. Citizen through acquisition.

CHOOSING AN ATTORNEY

Interviewer: What would you look for in an immigration attorney?

Paris Lee: I strongly feel that immigration is a specialty. If I had an immigration problem, I wouldn't be going to a generalist – somebody who does, for example, criminal defense, personal injury, divorce law, and also immigration. Immigration is constantly evolving every day. You have to keep up with new developments. It's something that, in my humble opinion, you really have to devote yourself to exclusively. If I had an immigration problem, I would go to somebody who practices only immigration law. That's number one. Number two: I would look for somebody who practices in the field that you actually have an issue with. For example, if I were looking for somebody to help me file for my wife, I wouldn't necessarily go to somebody who does immigration but only concentrates in employment-based cases. I would look for somebody who is going to concentrate on family-based cases. That's another consideration as well.

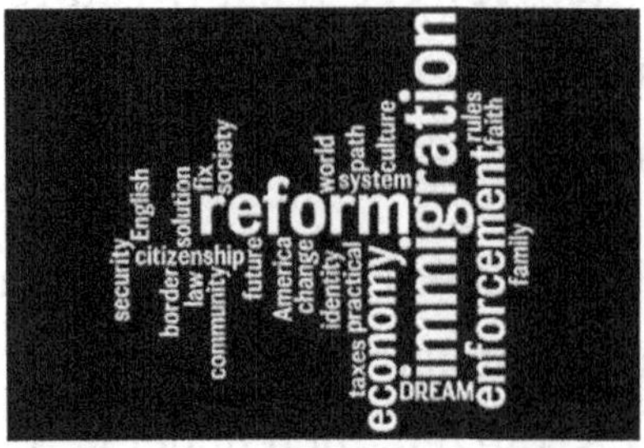

Then as far as what I'm looking for in an attorney, I want to look for somebody who has been practicing for quite a number of years, and who has practical experience dealing with the issue that I'm facing. Also, I want somebody who's going to be accessible to me. When I take on a case, I make it a point to educate my clients and speak to them in layman's terms so that they know exactly what's going on and what they have to do as well. I run across a lot of people in consultations who have had terrible attorneys. When I ask them what the other attorney did or what the strategy was, they have no idea!

Interviewer: What do you think they were told? "Just let me handle and don't worry about it."

Paris Lee: Yes, probably, but it's very important that the client have a clear understading of what the strategy is, what the law is, what the attorney can do, and what the attorney cannot do. I try to make the process as transparent as possible because in a way, undertaking an immigration case is like entering into a partnership. There is going to be a lot of work that I have to do, but I also need a lot of participation and input from the client as well.

Interviewer: Yes, because your cases, it seems, involve very deep issues that probably go on for a long time.

Paris Lee: Exactly, especially for hardship cases where we have to file waivers. When we're talking about what kind of hardship somebody is going to suffer – I can't make these things up. I have to know what's going on in that person's life. I have to know how that person is going to suffer if their loved one is not going to be able to stay here. I need input, so naturally, the client has to understand what needs to be proved.

Personal Statement

Interviewer: What sets you apart? What would you say sets you apart from other immigration attorneys and makes you particularly suited to help people?

Paris Lee: We have been practicing for close to 17 years. It's me and my partner Angie Garasia, who is the real superstar of the firm. The thing that makes us different is for the areas that we practice, we personally accompany and represent the client at the interview to ensure and mazimize the likelihood of a successful resolution. We have one attorney in the office – myself. I oversee the cases and I handle client's cases and emergencies as they arise. We're always accessible to our clients. Then we have my partner Angie who goes to immigration on a weekly basis, if not daily sometimes. She knows the local policies and procedures and understands what works and what doesn't.

That's very important. Basically what I'm saying is that my practice is more than just being able to tell you what you can find for yourself in a book or look up on the Internet. Of course, we have the knowledge; we know what the law says, but we also have a practical insight into how things really work as well. We go there all the time so we know what the local practice is as well as what the law allows. We use that combination to get the best for our clients.

Interviewer: In terms of personal experience, have you or your partners or associates gone through immigration-type experiences yourselves?

Paris Lee: My partner, yes. She immigrated here when she was a young child and went through the process. I have staff here who also went through the process firsthand. In fact, I helped file for my paralegal's husband to immigrate here. We helped him become a citizen so yes, we're intimately acquainted with the immigration process on a personal level as well. We have a high volume practice but at the same time, we try to make things as personal as possible. We know who our clients are. We deal mostly with individuals. We don't deal as much with larger companies. We serve individuals and their families. We make it a point to know each client's case on a personal level.

DISCLAIMER

This publication is intended to be informational only. No legal advice is being given, and no attorney-client relationship is intended to be created by reading this material. If you are facing legal issues, please seek professional legal counsel to get your questions answered.

LEE & GARASIA, LLC.

190 State Route 27
Edison, NJ 08820
(732) 516-1717
(888) 404-5876

www.njimmigrationattorney.com

Made in the USA
Monee, IL
04 November 2026

67386599R00030